CHURCH
MUSICIAN'S
GUIDE

BY
WAYNE GILPIN

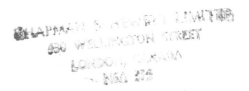

THE FREDERICK HARRIS MUSIC CO., LTD.
OAKVILLE, ONTARIO

Canadian Cataloguing in Publication Data

Gilpin, Wayne, 1947-
    Church Musician's Guide

ISBN 0-88797-191-1

Copyright© 1985 Wayne Gilpin

Published by The Frederick Harris Music Co., Limited
            529 Speers Road
            Oakville, Ontario L6K 2G4

Printed in Canada
F.H. 8536

Preface

This book has been written after an eighteen year tenure in the churches of this nation. Out of my experiences comes a volume of suggestions on how to get a job and organize a church music program, repertoire (Canadian) and ideas for developing musical growth in the church. It is a book for beginner and old-timer alike. I hope you find it interesting reading and of some value to your situation.

Wayne Gilpin

TABLE OF CONTENTS

CHAPTER FIVE: Professional Development and Miscellany

CHAPTER ONE:
Getting the Job

WHERE TO LOOK

1.   The local newspaper may list church positions under Help Wanted-Professional (hopefully!) or under Musical/Entertainment.

2.   Religious denominations publish internal news bulletins which list church positions under ads for Personnel Required. A postcard to any of the following will get you a sample bulletin or information on subscribing:

> United Church of Canada
> 85 St. Clair Ave. E.
> Toronto, Ontario
> M4T 1M8

> Presbyterian Church of Canada
> 50 Wynford Drive
> Don Mills, Ontario

> Anglican Book Centre
> 600 Jarvis Street
> Toronto, Ontario
> M4Y 2J6

3.   Two professional organizations can supply you with information on church positions. Contact:

> Royal Canadian College of Organists
> 500 University Ave.
> Suite 614
> Toronto, Ontario
> M5G 1V7

> American Guild of Organists
> 630 Fifth Ave.
> New York, New York
> 10020

RESUME WRITING

Once you have found a position for which you wish to apply, a resume should be sent. Your future career could well depend upon how masterful you are at resume writing. The resume provides the first impression for a prospective employer and first impressions count!

Your resume is, in condensed form, the story of your life. It should contain details of education, training, experience, work history, awards, and professional associations. The resume should contain everything noteworthy about your life, from your first piano teacher, through positions of responsibility held, to your unique talents.

As well as musical training and experience, fluency in languages, ability to operate office equipment, summer jobs, high school activities you enjoyed, all say something about you, and you never know what will interest or impress an interviewer. When I applied for a position as Director of Music at a church in Edmonton, my participation in public speaking contests many, many years before was remarked upon and was a mark in my favour. So put everything down.

Your complete submission might take the following form: cover letter, data sheet, chronology, summary, and documentation.

1.   COVER LETTER

Your cover letter should be in proper business letter format. Any guide to writing letters will show you this style of letter writing. I use an old high school text, *Mastering Effective English,* which has an excellent chapter on the subject. Use a good quality bond paper for your letter (and all pages of the resume).

Your cover letter will state that you are applying for a specific position and that you are enclosing a summary of your qulifications and experience. Your letter may go on to highlight, in a few sentences, your related experiences or particular competence for the position. See Appendix B for a sample letter.

2.   DATA SHEET

This sheet appears under the cover of your resume. (This cover is just a sheet of paper with the following centred on it: Summary of the Qualifications and Experience of [Your Name]). See Appendix A. The data sheet merely gives some statistics and family background about you and enables the employer to get a general picture and the information necessary to contact you. Include a recent photograph on this page. See Appendix C.

3.   CHRONOLOGY

The main part of the resume is a chronological listing of the main events in your life: schooling, activities, jobs, skills developed, hobbies. Some entries require a descriptive sentence to fully document the activity. See Appendix D.

4.   SUMMARY

This section summarizes the chronology by activities or type of job, etc., so that the employer can see at a glance how much experience of training you have had in a certain area. See Appendix E.

5.   DOCUMENTATION

Your neatly-typed, well-organized resume will have created a good impression and the documentation section should cinch the job. This section might include sample programmes you have performed, copies of certificates and awards you have received, newspaper clippings, reviews, tapes, or pictures.

6.   A WORD ABOUT REFERENCES

Most employers require fresh letters of reference when you apply. It is not necessary to give references on your application unless they are specifically requested. Merely state that references will be supplied on request.

Be sure to check with people you intend to list as a reference and ask them point-blank if they will give a favourable report. I once put down a Minister's name, a man with whom I had worked closely for two years, assuming he would give me a good reference, as I had been more than exemplary in the performance of my duties as Director of Music in his church. After being snubbed by two prospective employers, I was informed by a third that this person was defaming me and I realized that he had possibly cost me the first two jobs. Check your references!

THE INTERVIEW

SOME TIPS TO REMEMBER:

1.   Look your best.
2.   Answer all questions honestly.
3.   Express yourself clearly and confidently.
4.   Prepare some questions yourself regarding the job.
5.   At the end of the interview, thank the interviewers for their time and ascertain when you may expect to hear from them.

THE CONTRACT

Most churches will have a simple contract which will detail remuneration, duties, and benefits. The contract below, taken from the AGO booklet, The Work and Compensation of the Church Musician, should serve as a model. Naturally, it should be adapted to the individual situation. See Appendix F.

SALARY

The chart in Appendix G will show some suggested salary ranges for training and time spent on the job. Church music remuneration varies according to the vagaries of the church board, the social level in which the church is situated, the financial health of the congregation, the work expected from the church musician and the level of remuneration of other church musicians in the area.

In calculating the hours spent, the church musician should consider the following:

1.   Total time spent in the church building for Sunday services, special services, regular rehearsals, special rehearsals, preparing organ music for church use, organ maintenance, meetings.

2.   Time spent outside the church selecting music, learning the music, writing music for the choir, attendance at courses and workshops, preparing organ music, recruiting new members.

Church musicians in Canada are underpaid and underappreciated. The chart is more of an ideal than a reality. In my eighteen years of church music experience I have never managed to earn more than the church janitor. In one instance where I queried this, I was informed that "janitors are hard to come by."

CONFERRING WITH PREVIOUS DIRECTOR

If at all possible, hold a conference with the previous Director. He can give you some insight into the situation in the church. A discussion of specific vocal problems, prior repertoire (what the choir liked), what the congregation is used to, special music used in the church service, where all the resources of the church are kept, the names of key people in the church organization — all this can be gleaned from such a conference. You will then be better prepared and not greet your new position as a totally unknown situation.

THE BUILDING

Do some snooping around the building. Find out what all the rooms are used for and investigate their possibilities for musical events, rehersals or concerts. Ponder the organ/choir loft arrangement and decide if any changes are possible or desirable. Obtain keys for the building, church office and any rooms you wish to use.

THE ORGAN

Spend time becoming familiar with the instrument you will be using. If there are booklets pertaining to the organ, study them carefully. Take time to learn the colouration so that your registration may be most effective. An assessment of the mechanical condition of the organ should be forwarded regularly to the music and property committees.

THE RESOURCES

Know how much money is in the music budget and the procedure for ordering materials. Find out what electronic equipment is available for use (record player, projectors, tape recorders, microphones). Find out what duplicting services are available (spirit, gestetner, xerox). Is there other office equipment available? (Typewriter, staplers, folding machine). Go carefully through the choral music library and make a list of items to be used or ignored.

THE PEOPLE

1.   THE MINISTER

You will be responsible to the Minister in most church situations. Your relationship and rapport with him will depend on your respective personalities and concept of the place of music in the church. The Minister may be:

a)   totally disinterested in how you run the music programme. His only concern will be picking the hymns (and this should really be done in consultation between the Minister and the Music Director)

b)   interested in and supportive of the music programme, promoting it and working with you in a cooperative spirit (even going so far as to sing in the choir).

c)   critical of the music programme and constantly trying to undermine the contribution of music to church life.

May you be blessed with either a) or b). I have experienced all three.

2.   THE MUSIC COMMITTEE

The Music Committee should be an active support to the church musician. It should act as a personnel relations/ music programme liaison group to the Board of the church. Regular meetings with Music Director, Music Committee and the choir executive are a must. The Music Committee can support the church musician in matters of salary, special requests to the Board and the guidance of the total music programme.

3.   THE CHURCH SECRETARY

The church secretary can be of great assistance to you or none at all. It is a matter of personality and available time. In general, be nice to the secretary and she will be nice to you.

4.   THE CHOIR MEMBERS

The choir members will greet you with a variety of attitudes. Most choir members regard you with curiosity, neutrality, and a willingness to meet you half-way. Then there are the others. I have had: a long-time choir member walk out of my first rehearsal because she could not adjust to the new regime; a choir member refuse to cooperate and attempt to thwart my every suggestion because she desperately favoured the previous director. As if personality problems were not enough, you will have to face such vocal problems as tone-deaf basses, shrill and ill-tuned tenors, inaudible altos and widely vibrating sopranos. Hopefully, the previous director will have forewarned you. Once you have come to terms with the status quo you can go on to build your own programme.

CHAPTER TWO
Building Your Own Programme

RECRUITING

There are many useful avenues for increasing membership in church music organizations but the best one is personal contact.

1.   Get a list of the church membership and telephone or visit those members who are parents and invite them to bring their children out to the appropriate choir practice.

2.   Approach former choir members or get a line on musical people in the church and urge them to attend choir rehearsal.

3.   Have the Music Committee act as scouts for good voices in the congregation and approach these people yourself.

4.   Prepare a newsletter to be mailed out to church members detailing the musical activities available to all members of the family.

5.   Ask the Minister to make appeals from the pulpit for new members (or do it yourself!)

6.   Insert musical questionnaires or surveys in the Sunday bulletin.

7.   Dramatize the importance of the choir by having each member leave in turn during an anthem until only two or three people are left singing (shades of Haydn!) Follow this with an appeal for new members.

8.   Try the Family Sunday device. For one rehearsal and one service a family (mom, dad, and kids) from the church is invited to be temporary choir members. Hopefully, a taste of the experience will encourage them to become regular participants in the church music programme.

THE CHURCH MUSIC SYSTEM

Many churches run a junior and a senior choir and little else. The following suggested system represents a more complete programme.

CHOIRS:

Primary Choir (Ages 5-7)
Junior Choir (Ages 8-12)
High School Choir (Ages 13-17)
Senior Choir (Ages 18 and over)

OTHER GROUPS:

Handbell Choir
Recorder Group
Instrumental Groups
Mens and Ladies Choirs

This type of programme would obviously entail a full-time position. It would provide a continuous programme of choir development and also give those with other musical interests a chance to participate as well.

1.   PRIMARY CHOIR

These little children could be brought by their parents to the church for weekly rehearsals sometime during the day. Each rehearsal would last for half an hour and be used for musical games, teaching simple tunes, and introducing the children to being in a choir. The programme might be augmented by attendance at a Junior Choir rehearsal for observation, and certainly the children would perform for the congregation two or three times during the year. Investigate the Kodaly (Threshold to Music — Mary Helen Richards) and Orff (Music for Children) concepts of music education for young children. At this level, music should be fun!

2. JUNIOR CHOIR

Weekly rehearsals of one hour are recommended for this group. They should perform once a month during a church service and rehearsals should be used for preparation for this performance and for learning about music. Instruction sheets on music, words to songs, a place for stars for attendance and other sheets should be kept by each singer in a three-ring notebook — a Junior Choir book. Extra activities could include performances in the community (hospitals, old age homes, community events) or a trip to a special musical event (choir concert, symphony concert).

3. HIGH SCHOOL CHOIR

This group rehearses for one to two hours weekly, probably on Sunday afternoon is best. A special service could be undertaken or a special concert planned (folk mass, innovative Christmas pageant). Young people in this age group require a special rapport and special motivation to maintain their interest during the teen years.

4. THE SENIOR CHOIR

This choir meets once weekly for two hours, usually on a Wednesday or Thursday evening. Besides leading the congregation during the service and providing special music in the form of anthems, the senior group can provide the nucleus of an outreach group into the community.

5. INSTRUMENTAL GROUPS

The handbell and recorder groups, as well as other instrumental groups are used to support the choirs, or occasionally to perform on their own. The Director should arrange hymns and musical accompaniments for these groups.

6. MENS AND LADIES CHOIRS

These groups investigate a more restricted repertoire and may attract people who do not wish to join the mixed groups. These groups can be more flexible about when they meet.

ADMINISTERING THE CHOIR

1. GETTING TO KNOW YOU...

a)   Information Form

At the first meeting with the choir, have them fill out a form for basic information. A choir is a human endeavour and you should know something about the people singing for you. The information may be entered on sheets or cards and the data thus collected will help you learn names of choristers, something of their background, and how to contact them. (See Appendix H for a sample information card)

b)   The Audition

The audition is the time to chat with the chorister and to evaluate musical qualities. Use the audition to begin a friendly relationship with your choir. Make the audition as non-threatening as possible. Simply pick a mutually suitable time to meet with the chorister and have them sing a song or a hymn they know. Make a note of any musical pluses or minuses.

c)   Capsule Biography

A device I have used is to have each chorister stand, give their name, and tell something about their background. It helps to break the ice.

2. *ATTENDANCE*

   a)   Propaganda

   Hand out a propaganda card at the first rehearsal. (See appendix I)

   b)   Keeping Records

   Keep a record of everyone's attendance at both rehearsals, services and concerts using some type of form. (See Appendix J for a sample form).

   c)   Postcards

   Make use of choir postcards to remind choristers of rehearsals or concerts or that you missed them at rehearsal. Let them know you care. (See Appendix K for some sample cards)

   d)   Telephone

   Often a quick telephone call will make all the difference: the chorister calling to apologize for a missed rehearsal, the conductor inquiring after reported illness or whatever. Keep in touch.

   e)   Incentives

   Choir awards (pins, gift books, certificates, etc.) may improve attendance, morale, and attitudes. Consider them.

3. *SEATING*

   a)   Physical Set-up

   Unless your seating arrangement is fixed (Church pews, etc.) seat your choristers in a "U" formation where they can hear each section of the choir and see the conductor.

   b)   Each to his own...

   Once you have seated your choristers for best blend and compatibility, indicate to the choir that they now occupy that seat for the season. It is important to have a place of one's own (your choir morale will escalate) and it is a handy attendance check when you see those empty seats.

4. *MUSIC*

   a)   Folder

   Each chorister should have a folder with his/her name on it in which is contained all necessary music, choir regulations, rehearsal pencil, kleenex, pocketbook, lipstick, bandaids, sunglasses, etc. The folder is retained by the chorister on the theory that if they take it home between rehearsals, they might actually look at the music between rehearsals. The choir librarian can be responsible for keeping the music in the folder up to date, removing old numbers, inserting new ones.

   b)   Storage

   Filing folders and cabinets are usually sufficient for most choral libraries. If you are using more than 25 copies, consider choral index boxes made of cardboard. The boxes are stored vertically on shelves and really protect the music.

   c)   File Cards

   Keep a complete and up-to-date set of file cards on the music. Each piece of music should be numbered as it is purchased and stored in numerical order. The file cards will index each piece as to composer, title, resources, etc. Keep a list (shelf list) of the library in numerical order for reference. (See Appendix L for sample file cards.)

5.   CHOIR EXECUTIVE

Elect a choir executive and then make it function to take over those duties (care of music, correspondence, fund raising, social activities) that will leave you free to concentrate on the artistic end of things.

President — Over-all responsibility for functions of choir.
Secretary — Handles all correspondence and minutes of meetings.
Treasurer — Handles all monies, credit and debit.
Librarian — Files, distributes, cares for music.
Manager — Handles lighting, seating, physical aspects
Uniforms — Care and repair of gowns.
Social — Organizes social events for choir members
Attendance Secretary — Takes attendance at rehearsals, services and special events.

6.   CHOIR MOTHERS

The mothers of the primary and junior choirs form a loosely-knit organization to help supervise and promote choir rehearsals, Sunday performances and other choir activities.

7.   ATTITUDE TO CHOIR

Picture #1: Conductor arrives minutes late, slowly removes coat, heaves music down with a sigh and groans to the choir, complaining of fatigue.
Picture #2: Conductor arrives half an hour early to check set-up, greets choristers bang on the rehearsal hour with a cheery greeting, and in a spirited manner asks them to turn to the first piece of music (or starts warm-up).

8.   FINANCES

Money rears its ugly head and many choir programmes are stunted and enthusiastic leaders frustrated by the lack of funds. So take the bull by the horns and raise that money you need.
Raising Money: car wash, selling Christmas cards, putting on concerts, putting on dances, making and selling a recording, selling chocolate, importune rich people, government grants.

PLANNING FOR THE YEAR

Block out the whole year for each group on a chart. The sample in Appendix M is for Senior Choir.

CHAPTER THREE
Repertoire

Do you repeat anthems frequently? Are you happy to do the same Christmas numbers each year? Have you expanded your own knowledge of choral conducting requirements? Does your repertoire and that of your choir extend before Bach/Handel and after Mozart? Does your choir library contain Buck, Simper, Shaw, Thiman to the exclusion of Dufay, Bach, Brahms, Dello Joio? When was the last time you were enthusiastic about a choir rehearsal? Are your rehearsals planned, or conducted on a wing and a prayer? Growth is the key.

The following is a selection of much fine Canadian sacred music available (but not as well utilized as it should be!) This music is of excellent quality and should find a place in every choir's library.

JUNIOR CHOIRS (Primary and Junior Choirs)

1.   GENERAL

Anderson, W.H.	A Child's Prayer (Unison)	Leslie 1006
Bissell, Keith	Rejoice Today With One Accord (Unison)	Harris HC1005
Clarke, F.R.C.	Lord Of All Hopefulness, Lord Of All Joy (2 Part)	Waterloo
Day, Peggy	As The Branch Is To The Vine (2 Part)	Leslie 2048
	Gentle Father (2 Part)	Leslie 2049
France, William	A Child's Prayer To The Shepherd (SA)	Harris HC2006
	Hear Us, Holy Jesus (SA)	Harris HC2007
	Jesu, Tender Shepherd, Hear Us (Unison)	Harris HC1007
	Loving Shepherd Of Thy Sheep (2 Part)	Harris
	A Morning Hymn (SA)	Harris HC2002
MacLennan, Robert	Jesu, Tender Shepherd (SA)	Waterloo
Martindale, James	A Morning Prayer An Evening Prayer (2 Part)	Leslie 2047
Watson, Ruth	I Will Extol Thee (Unison)	Waterloo
Willan, Healey	Fairest Lord Jesus (SA)	Peters 6233
	Jesus, Good Above All Other (SA)	Peters 6676
Younger, John	The Lamb (2 Part)	Harris HC2001

2.   CHRISTMAS

Anderson, W.H.	The Birth-Night (2 Part)	Leslie 1008
	Carol O Ye Angels (2 Part)	Leslie 2012
	Long, Long Ago (Unison)	Leslie 1030
	Mary (Unison)	Leslie 429
	Sleep Little Jesus (Unison)	Leslie 1010
	'Twas In The Silent Night He Came (Unison)	Leslie 1069

Bissell, Keith	In Bethlehem (Unison)	Waterloo
Harrhy, Edith	Ring, Bells, Ring (Unison) HC1008	Harris
Hill, Harry	A Christmas Lullaby (Unis.)	Waterloo
	Dear Little Stranger (Unis.)	Waterloo
	Out On A Hillside & Bright Shone The Star (Unis.)	Waterloo
Kemp, Walter	Three Xmas Songs: Christmas-Tide Rejoicing Jesus Was Once A Child Like Me Of A Birth Sing We (U)	Waterloo
Kruspe, Glenn	This New Christmas Carol (SA)	Waterloo
Slater, David Dick	The Little Lord Jesus (2 Part)	Harris

3. COLLECTIONS

Bissell, Keith	O Come Let Us Sing (18 Anthems For The Church Year)		Waterloo
Fox, George	Seven Simple Sacred Songs		Harris
Grimes, Travis	Lift Up Your Heads! (10 Unison Chorales)		Waterloo
Kruspe, Glenn	King of Glory (15 Anthems)		Waterloo
MacNutt, Walter	The Waterloo Book Of Hymns And Descants (16 Well-Known Hymns, Unis. With Descant)		Waterloo
Ritchey, Lawrence	Twelve Unison Anthems		Waterloo
Willan, Healey	Carols For The Seasons (22 Carols)	97-6319	Concordia
	We Praise Thee I	97-7564	Concordia
	We Praise Thee II	97-7610	Concordia

4. EXTENDED WORKS

Feltmate, Peggy and Howard Cable	Your Work With Love Surrounds You (A Cantata: The Creation For Children — 15 Min.)	Boston

SENIOR CHOIRS
(High School Choir, Senior Choir, Men's and Ladies)
(All SATB Unless Otherwise Noted)

1. INTROITS

Archer, Violet	Introit And Choral Prayer	C264	BMI
Baker, Richard C.	Three Short Introits	HC4057	Harris
Russell, Welford	Eleven Introits For All Seasons		Leeds

Tapscott, Carl	Six Hymn Introits	Waterloo
Willan, Healey	Introits For Festival And General Use	Leslie 4069

2. ALL SAINTS'

Betts, Lorne	The Souls Of The Righteous	Waterloo
Lapp, Horace	O Lamb Of God	Waterloo
Meek, Kenneth	The Song Of The Fathers	Leslie 4092

3. THANKSGIVING

Anderson, W.H. (Arr.)	O Lord Of All ("Largo" From "Xerxes")	Leslie 4043
Clark, Henry A.	Praise To God, Immortal Praise	Leslie 4109
Slater, David Dick	Prayer Of Thanksgiving (Old Dutch Melody)	Harris HC4061
Whitehead, Alfred	Golden Grain, Harvest Bringing	Boston 1860
Willan, Healey	God Of Mercy (Hymn-Anthem On "Heathlands")	Peters 6989
	I Will Give Thanks	Concordia 98-1554
	Now Thank We All Our God (Hymn-Anthem On "Nun Danket")	Peters 6588
	Rejoice, O Land (Hymn-Anthem On "Wareham")	Peters 6986
	Sing To The Lord Of Harvest 98-2013 SATB 98-1450 SSA 98-1451 SAB 98-1454 JR.-SR. Combined Choirs 98-1643 SA.-JR. Choir With Descant 97-4501 - 97-4507 Brass Ensemble	Concordia

4. CHRISTMAS

A) SAB

Bissell, Keith	Lo! He Comes With Clouds Descending	Waterloo
Morgan, Hilda (Arr.)	Whence Is That Goodly Frangrance?	Waterloo
Powell, Wilfred (Arr.)	Masters In This Hall	Harris HC3002

B) SSA

Anderson, W.H.	The Lullaby Of The Little Angels	GVT E.I. 1003
Hill, Harry (Arr.)	What Is This Fragrance?	Waterloo
	Lo! How A Rose E'er Blooming	Waterloo
Ouchterlony, David	There Came A Star	Harris HC2005
Rogers, Wm. Keith	Two Christmas Carols	BMI

C) Arrangements (SATB)

Applebaum, Louis	Cherry Tree Carol (Canadian)	Leeds

Clark, Henry A.	Good Christian Men, Rejoice	Leslie 4110
Hassell, Desmond	Love Came Down At Christmas (Irish)	Waterloo
MacNutt, Walter	The Golden Carol (R. Vaughan Williams)	Waterloo

Whitehead, Alfred	Three Christmas Carols
	    Dear Nightingale. Awake!
	    The Christ-Child Smiles
	    Come In, Dear Angels
		Leslie 4004

	Three Christmas Carols
	    O Little Christ Sweet
	     (S. Scheidt)
	    O Gay Is The Day We Sing
	     (Provencal)
	    The Carol Of The Good
	     Thief (Dutch)
		Leslie 4008

Willan, Healey	Christmas Song Of The XIVth Century	Leeds
	From The Eastern Mountains (Montes Orientis)	Oxford
	Hosanna To The Living Lord (Von Himmel Hoch)	Concordia 98-2004
	Lift Up Your Heads, Ye Mighty Gates (Macht Hoch Die Tur)	Concordia 98-2003
	Lo! He Comes With Clouds Descending	Concordia 98-1592
	What Is This Lovely Fragrance? (Old French)	GVT G-589
Wilson, Charles	The Cherry Tree Carol (English)	Waterloo
Younger, John B.	An Echo Carol (Old French)	Harris HC4067

D) EDITIONS

Bach, J.S.
(Ed. Beran)
	Two Chorales From "Christmas Oratorio":
	    Break Forth
	    Ah Dearest Jesus
		Waterloo

E) ORIGINAL COMPOSITIONS

Anderson, W.H.	As I Walked In Bethlehem	Leslie 4057
	Christmas Questionings	Leslie 4018
	The Holy Child	Harris

	Two Christmas Carols
	    Carol. O Ye Angels
	    A Quiet Chamber
		Leslie 4015

	Two Christmas Carols
	    A Wassail Song
	    Cradle Hymn
		Leslie 4016

	Two Christmas Carols	Leslie 4017
Bissell, Keith	Welcome Yule	Waterloo
Hill, Harry	Calm Was The Night	Waterloo
	Unto Us A Boy Is Born	Leslie 4107
Klusmeier, Ron	Christmas Message	Harmuse HC4058
	Gift of New Sight	Harmuse HC4059
Kunz, Alfred	Sweet Child Of God	Waterloo
MacLennan, Robert	O Lord My Babe Foretold	Waterloo
Morgan, Hilda	This Little Babe	Waterloo
Ouchterlony, David	There Came A Star	Harris HC4025
Wallace, William	The Ox And The Donkey's Carol	Harris 4001
Whitehead, Alfred	Bell Carol	Boston 1771
	The Bird Carol	Boston 1770
Willan, Healey	Arise, Shine, For Thy Light Is Come	Concordia 98-1508
	The Story Of Bethlehem	Concordia 97-7572

5. LENT

| Crueger-Bach-Bissell | Ah. Holy Jesu | Waterloo |
| Willan, Healey | Behold The Lamb Of God | Concordia 98-1509 |

6. PALM SUNDAY

Silvester, Frederick	Ride On, Ride On In Majesty	Harris
Willan, Healey	Hosanna To The Son Of David	Concordia 98-1016
	Rejoice, Ye Pure In Heart! (Marion)	Peters 6065

7. EASTER

Bissell, Keith	Christ, Being Raised From The Dead	GVT G-537
	Christ Is Risen From The Dead	Waterloo
Clark, Henry A.	Alleluia, Christ Is Risen	Leslie 4111
	He Is Risen	Leslie 4108
Gosse, Barry (Arr.)	This Joyful Eastertide (Dutch Carol)	Waterloo
Whitehead, Alfred	Earth Today Rejoices (Piae Cantiones)	Boston 1632
	Now Easter Is Here (Welsh Carol)	Boston 1633
Willan, Healey	Christ Our Passover	Concordia 98-1009
	God Is Gone Up With A Shout	Concordia 98-1543
	We Sing The Praise Of Him Who Died	Peters 6224
	Worthy Art Thou, O God	Concordia 98-1015
Younger, John B.	Now Is Christ Risen	Harris

8. COMMUNION

France, William	O Jesu, Blessed Lord	Waterloo
Hill, Harry (Arr.)	Let Us Break Bread (Negro Spiritual)	Waterloo
Morgan, Hilda	Communion Hymn	Waterloo
Ouchterlony, David	O Food Of Men Wayfaring	Harris HC4035
Whitehead, Alfred	Jesus, Bread Of Life, I Pray Thee	Leslie 4003
Willan, Healey	Let All Mortal Flesh Keep Silence (Picardy)	Peters 6262
	O Sacred Feast	Leeds 715
Younger, John B.	Be Known To Us	Harris HC4005

9. GENERAL
A) SAB

Brandon, George	The Lord Is King	Augsburg APM-461
Clark, Henry A.	Breathe On Me, Breath Of God	Harris HC3003

B) SSA

Dawson, J.A.	O Give Thanks Unto The Lord	Waterloo
Hill, Harry (Arr.)	Let Us Break Bread (Negro Spiritual)	Waterloo

C) EDITIONS

Ford. Thomas (Ed. Bevan)	Almight God, Who Hast Me Brought	Waterloo
Hilton, John (Ed. Sweetman)	The Lamentations Of Jeremiah	Waterloo
	Lord, For Thy Tender Mercies' Sake	Waterloo
Lawes, Henry (Ed. Sweetman)	Thou And Thy Wond'rous Deeds, O Lord	Waterloo
Mendelssohn, Felix (Ed. Bevan)	Four Chorales From "Saint Paul"	Waterloo
Mozart, W.A. (Ed. Bevan)	Ave Verum	Waterloo
Tye, Christopher (Ed. Bevan)	O Come, Ye Servants Of The Lord	Waterloo

D) ARRANGEMENTS AND HYMN-ANTHEMS

Brandon, George	Stand Up For Jesus (Anonymous Tune)	Waterloo
O'Neill, Dr. Charles	Onward Christian Soldiers (Sir Arthur Sullivan)	Waterloo
White, Herbert D.	Jesus, Jesus (Wollt Ihr Wissen Was Mein Preis)	Waterloo
Whitehead, Alfred	Come Sweet Evening Guest (Seelenbrautigan, Jesu, Gotteslamm)	Boston 1914

	Evening Hymn (Nun Ruhen Alle Wälder)	Boston 1984
	Soldiers Of Christ, Arise! (Harmonica Sacra)	Boston 1869
Willan, Healey	Before Jehovah's Awe-Full Throne (Old Hundredth)	Peters 6239
	Christ, Whose Glory Fills The Skies (Ratisbon)	Concordia 98-2006
	Father Of Heaven, Whose Love Profound (Angelus)	Concordia 98-2005
	Father, We Praise Thee (Christe Sanctorum)	Peters 6125
	Guide Me, O Thou Great Redeemer (St. Osmund)	Peters 6157
	Jesus, Lead Thou On (Seelenbrautigan)	Concordia 98-2035
	Let All The World In Every Corner Sing	Peters 6677
	Lord Of All Hopefullness (Slane)	Peters 6985
	O Strength And Stay (Donne Secours)	Peters 6126
	O Trinity Of Blessed Light (St. Venantius)	Peters 6252
	O What Their Joy And Their Glory Must Be (O Quanta Qualia)	Peters 6066
	Praise To The Lord (Lobe Den Herren)	Peters 6266
	Rise, Crowned With Light (Old 124th)	Concordia 98-2001
	Strengthen For Service, Lord The Hands (Ach Gott Und Herr)	Peters 6510
	Through The Day Thy Love Has Spared Us (St. Leonard)	Peters 6400
	Ye Watchers And Ye Holy Ones	Peters 6238
Younger, John B.	My Song Is Love Unknown (ChristChurch)	Harris HC4026
	O God Of Bethel!	Harris HC4032

E)   ORIGINAL COMPOSITIONS

Anderson, W.H.	The Beatitudes	GVT G-585
	Give Ear To My Words, O Lord	Leslie 4035
Archer, Violet	I Will Lift Up Mine Eyes	Waterloo
Bancroft, Hugh	Love Of The Father	Leslie 4009
	O Be Joyful In The Lord	Waterloo
	O Thou Not Made With Hands	Leslie 4101

Bissell, Keith	Hear Thou My Prayer, O Lord	GVT G-544
	I Was Glad When They Said Unto Me	Waterloo
Chubb, Frederick	O Send Out Thy Light	Leslie 4090
Clark, Henry A.	Bow Down Thy Ear	Harris
	Come, Holy Ghost	Harris
	Come Unto Me	Harris
	I Will Praise The Name Of The Lord	Harris
	Jubilate Deo	Harris HC4011
	Let Not Your Heart Be Troubled	Harris HC4012
	Let Thy Merciful Ears, O Lord	Harris
Clarke, F.R.C.	Father We Praise Thee (Unison and Descant)	Waterloo
	Hail, Thou Source Of Every Blessing	Waterloo
	Lord Of Our Life (Unison and Descant)	Waterloo
	O Father On Our Festal Day	Waterloo
	With Joy We Go Up To The House Of The Lord	Waterloo
Dawson, J.A.	O Christ Who Holds The Open Gate	Waterloo
Eaton, R.S.	Blest Are The Pure In Heart	Waterloo
Fox, George	Christ Is Our Cornerstone	Waterloo
	In The Lord's Atoning Grief	Waterloo
France, William	Lord Jesus, Think On Me	Waterloo
	Lord Of All Power And Might	Harris
Hill, Harry	Psalm 23	Waterloo
Jerome, Howard K.	The Lord's Prayer	Harris
Kenins, Talivaldis	Psalm 150	Waterloo
Klusmeier, Ron	The Lord Is My Shepherd	Harmuse HC4063
	Man Is Not Alone	Harmuse HC4064
MacNutt, Walter	Jesu, Son Of Mary	Waterloo
	O Gladsome Light	Waterloo
Moss, Cyril	Jesu, Soul Of My Heart's Desire	Harris
	Let Thy Merciful Ears, O Lord	Harris
Ouchterlony, David	God Is Our Refuge And Strength	Harris HC1001
	Let Them That Say They Love The Lord	Harris HC4036
	Praise God!	Harris HC4023
	Trust In The Lord, And Do Good	GVT G-562
Ritchey, Lawrence	God Be In My Head	Waterloo

Silvester, Frederick	Be Merciful Unto Me	Harris
	Come, Ye Disconsolate	Harris
	I Will Give Thanks Unto The Lord	Harris
	Softly Now The Light Of Day	Harris
Watson, Ruth	O King Of Kings	Waterloo
Whitehead, Alfred	Come, Holy Ghost, In Love	Harris HC4008
	God Of Mercy, God Of Grace	Harris HC4004
	Hark The Song Of Jubilee	GVT G-583
	Let All The World In Every Corner Sing	Harris HC4019
	O Light, Beyond Our Utmost Light	Boston 1943
Willan, Healey	The Aaronic And Apostolic Benedictions	Peters 6099
	Ave Verum Corpus	Harris
	Blessed Art Thou, O Lord	GVT G-592
	Christ Hath A Garden	Harris HC4056
	Grant Us Thy Light	Concordia 98-1014
	Great Is The Lord	GVT G-590
	Hail, Gladdening Light	Leeds 712
	Holy, Holy, Holy Is The Lord	Concordia 98-1553
	I Will Lay Me Down In Peace	Concordia 98-1231
	I Will Lift Up Mine Eyes	Concordia 98-1017
	Let Us Worship And Fall Down	Leeds 717
	Like As The Hart	Concordia 98-1230
	Magnificat And Nunc Dimittis	Oxford 5534
	Missa De Sancta Maria Magdalena	Oxford S424
	O Be Joyful	GVT G-591
	O How Glorious	Leeds 713
	Recessional	Harris
	Rejoice, O Jerusalem, Behold, Thy King Cometh	Concordia 98-1506
	The Spirit Of The Lord	Concordia 98-1013
	Very Bread, Good Shepherd Tend Us	Leeds 714
	We Praise Thee, O God	Concordia 98-1126
Wilson, C.M.	And Now Bless The God Of All	Waterloo
Younger, John B.	The Lord Is My Strength And My Song	Harris HC4044
	O Heavenly Beauty	Harris
	There Is A Green Hill	Harris

10. EXTENDED WORKS

Bissell, Keith	Let There Be Joy (10 Min.) (Organ, Flute, Cello, Glock, Xyl.)	GVT

18

Cozens, John (Comp.)	The Road To Calvary (Readings From Holy Scriptures and Music Of Chorales Harmonized By J.S. Bach)	Concordia 98-1629
Ouchterlony, David	Carol Cantata (Christmas) (55 Min.)	Harris

11. COLLECTIONS

Ed. Jackson, Francis	Anthems For Choirs	Oxford
	The Church Anthem Book	Oxford
	Oxford Easy Anthem Book	Oxford

12. CONTEMPORARY CHURCH MUSIC

Wild, Eric	Hymn Sing	Harmuse
	Hymns For Now (Workers Quarterly)	
Klusmeier, Ron	Praise To The Lord!	Harmuse
	Rejoice!	Marks Music
Songs Of Faith	The Joint Board of Christian Education of Australia and New Zealand 147 Collins Street Melbourne, Victoria, Australia	
27 - 20th Century Hymns	Josef Weinberger Ltd. 10-16 Rathbone Street London W.1	

CANADIAN PUBLISHERS

Bernadol Music	11 St. Joseph St. Toronto M4Y 1J8
Frederick Harris	529 Speers Road Oakville L6K 2G4
E.C. Kerby Limited	198 Davenport Road Toronto M5R 1J2
Leslie Music Supply	Box 471 Oakville, Ontario L6J 5A8
G.V. Thompson Ltd.	29 Birch Ave. Toronto M4V 1B2
Waterloo Music	3 Regina St. N. Waterloo, Ontario N2J 4A5

CHAPTER FOUR
The Work of the Church Musician

REHEARSALS

1.   SCHEDULING

One rehearsal per week is the norm for most choirs, except when a special event is being prepared, in which case extra rehearsals would be scheduled. A Sunday morning pre-service rehearsal for the performing choir is useful. Use the time to warm up the voices, review the music to be sung (any changes made, some performance details, sing through parts of it or all of it) or provide some morale boosting.

2.   REHEARSAL ROUTINE

Choirs have a traditional routine which involves a period of rehearsal with a break for announcements or stretching, or an actual break for coffee or choir business. Consider using a fixed routine such as the following:

> Vocalizing warm-up
> Work on new music
> Review work of previous week
> Break
> Additional work on current repertoire
> Polishing Sunday's anthem
> End with a familiar piece

Be flexible and try to respond to the mood of the choir and the dynamics of the choral situation.

3.   REHEARSAL SUGGESTIONS

> Be inflexible about starting on time
> Be prepared with a written rehearsal plan
> Be succinct in what you say
> Do not allow choir to talk during rehearsing
> Keep in eye contact with choir
> Keep the pace going
> Be encouraging and sympathetic (but know when to be stern!)
> Isolate the specific choral problem, correct it, and replace in context. Do not just repeat phrases, hoping the problems will iron out.
> Ask the choir members to inform you of their problems
> Inject some humour to offset the intensive work of rehearsing
> Teach principles and not cases. Rather than telling the choir where to breathe in each specific instance, teach them how to decide where breath should or should not be taken, unless they receive specific instructions from the conductor.

4.   CHORAL PROBLEMS

a)   Breathing and Posture

Lack of breath and poor posture are prime church choir problems. An explanation of the breathing process, some breathing exercises to improve breath control and some common sense advice about breathing practices will all help. Make sense of the language, breathe usually at commas, never break up a word, use staggered breathing. Command or demand improved posture when singing.

b)   Intervals

Just learning the notes may be a problem. Isolate the two notes of the interval causing the problem and drill them five times in a row and the problem may be solved. Once the interval is secure, have the entire phrase sung two or three times to fix it in the choristers' minds.

c)   Rhythm

Train your choir to count properly and correct rhythmic problems by reducing the offending rhythmic figure to its lowest common denominator, dissecting it in effect, then replace it in context. For example:

 would be thought of as

d)   Intonation

Out of tune singing usually results from lack of control (of breath or vocal apparatus) or lack of knowledge of the harmonic basis of the work. The voice part singing the major third of the chord, for example, should tune up that chord. Use arrows (↑ ↓) to indicate subtle tuning of specific notes.

e)   Voice Problems

The church musician usually has to deal with a volunteer choir and may be confronted with some unpleasant voice problems. Weak voices, strident voices, excessive vibratos, poor pitching, nasal resonance, improper diction, all plague the director. The offending members will usually welcome some personal attention and individual help.

f)   Artistic Considerations

Attention to artistic and sensitive performance should apply equally to hymns and anthems. The expression and mood of the music must be reflected in the choir's performance.

SUNDAY SERVICE

The following is a step-by-step account of the work of the organist-choir director during a typical Sunday service.

Organ Prelude (The prelude should set a meditative mood. Open all music required on music stand, have call to worship or introit music at hand, have hymn book open to first hymn.)

Call to Worship (Said or sung)

Hymn of Praise (Play through hymn completely in correct tempo)

Prayer of Approach and Lord's Prayer (During prayer of approach get out music for Lord's Prayer and responsive reading)

Responsive Reading (If said, be prepared to launch into the Gloria if required to be sung at end)

The Pastoral Prayer (Prepare music for offertory, dedication and anthem)

The Offertory (When collection is over, be able to stop piece satisfactorily and modulate into chord or introductory phrase for offertory)

The Anthem (Have a definite signal, head or hand, to get choir up and a set routine for sitting together — everyone sits on final chord of accompaniment, for example)

Announcements (Prepare for next hymn)

Scripture Lesson

Hymn of the Gospel

Sermon (Prepare for last hymn, choral Amen, postlude)

Hymn of dedication

Benediction and Choral amen

Postlude (Try a quiet one for a change)

Do not try to fill in all the silences in the service.

Hymns should be sung with first and last verses in unison and other verses in harmony.

SPECIAL SERVICES AND CONCERTS

1.   Baptism — This service is usually included within the regular Sunday service. The only musical requirement may be the choir singing the Hebrew Benediction.

2.   Funerals — Appropriately solemn music when required.

3.   Weddings — Appropriately joyful music. Resist the temptation to be "current." Do not get too upset about people talking while you play.

4.   Communion — Quiet background music during the serving of the elements. Make use of the choir singing communion hymns or anthems.

5.   Festival Services — Pick festive music or extended works and use instrumentalists to give a special flavour to the service.

6.   Concerts — A year-end concert is a worthy goal for the complete church music programme. A sample programme may be found in Appendix N.

CHAPTER 5
Professional Development and Miscellany

ORGANIZATIONS

Consider joining the following:

Royal Canadian College of Organists
500 University Avenue
Suite 614
Toronto, Ontario
M5G 1V7

American Guild of Organists
630 Fifth Ave.,
New York, New York
10020

EXAMINATIONS

Organ examinations are conducted by the following:

Royal Conservatory of Music
273 Bloor Street W.
Toronto, Ontario

Western Board of Music
University of Alberta
Edmonton, Alberta

The AGO conducts four types of examination:

1. Service Playing
2. Choir Master
3. Associateship
4. Fellowship

The RCCO conducts:

1. Diploma of Fellowship
2. Diploma of Associateship
3. Choir-training Diploma
4. Certificate of Proficiency

PRIVATE TEACHING

The church may serve as a studio for private teaching by the church music director. Pupils may come from the choirs and instrumental groups, the congregation, or the general community. Private teaching is a necessary adjunct to the salary of the church musician.

HYMN-PLAYING

The tempo of the hymn should be chosen for musical rather than congregational reasons. The music should flow, whether stately or quickly, because there is a musical tempo range appropriate to the hymn. The following are some suggested tempos:

All Creatures of Our God and King ♩ = 116
(Lasst uns erfreuen)

All Things Bright and Beautiful ♩ = 138
(Royal Oak)

Be Thou My Vision (Slane) ♩ = 96

Fairest Lord Jesus (Crusader's Hymn) ♩ = 100

God Reveals His Presence (Arnsberg) ♩ = 104

O Master, Let me Walk with Thee (Maryton) ♩ = 126

Do not slow down at the end of every hymn.

Do not interject interludes between verses.

Do make use of faux-bourdon, descants and improvisations (Changed harmonies, added counterpoint)

Do vary the registration occasionally during the hymn.

CONDUCTING

A recommended textbook on conducting is *Conducting Technique* by Brock McElheran (Oxford). This book will give you a sound technical and philosophical basis. The organist-choir director will make much use of his head and eyes to lead the choir or use the right hand alone, the organ being carried by the left hand and the pedals.

THE ORGANIST

Make use of the best in organ repertoire. Study accompaniments as carefully as you would voluntaries. Know the organ registration and maintenance. Some suggested repertoire (Easy to Difficult):

Bach	Orgelbuchlein, Volume 15	Novello
	Eight Short Preludes and Fugues	Novello
Willan	Six chorale Preludes, Set I	Concordia
Ed. Bonnet	Historical Recitals, Vol I	Kalmus
Cabena	Cabena's Homage	Waterloo
Bach	The Little G Minor Fugue	Novello
Bohm	Prelude and Fugue in C	Peters
Mendelssohn	Sonata No. 5 in D	
Bingham	Baroques Suite	Galaxy

BOOKS ON THE ORGAN:

Alcock	The Organ	Novello
Jack C. Goode	Pipe Organ Registration	Abingdon

See Appendix O for a sample church musician's timetable.

OVERCOMING DESPAIR

We all despair at one time or another over our choir work. Re-examine your attitude, your programme, your approach, your planning, your follow-through, your artistic concepts. Talk to a fellow conductor, read an inspiring book, listen to a great piece of music, have a cup of tea.

A NOTE TO THE CONGREGATION ON HYMN SINGING

The psalmist tells us to "make a joyful noise unto the Lord." Our congregational hymn-singing must reflect this admonition, for many of the hymns are happy and can be sung joyfully. The following suggestions regarding hymn singing are offered in the spirit of praising with a smile.

Tempo:

The musical qualities of hymn tunes dictate a tempo that flows along. Musically, some of them could be described in dance terms, and should be played and sung that way.

Breathing:

Take a good breath before you start to sing and breathe at the end of sentences or where there is a logical break in the poetry. If the hymn is in the proper tempo, you won't have to breathe as often.

Words:

The words of a hymn must make sense. Unfortunately, the musical and grammatical phrases do not always match, so words may have to be carried beyond the musical phrase. If there is no comma at the end of the line of poetry, then no breath should be taken if the words are to be intelligible. For example:

This is My Father's World

This is my Father's world, (breathe at comma here)
and to my listening ears (musical phrase ends here but no comma so no breath)
All nature sings, (breathe here) and round me rings (no breath)
the music of the spheres. (Breathe at end of sentence)

The tendency to breathe after "ears" makes gibberish of the English meaning of the poetry.

Pauses:

If no pause is marked in the music then the music doesn't stop, but goes on. There may be a slight slowing at points to get a breath but the traditional pauses destroy the musical flow, and there is no reason to slow down on the last line of every hymn.

Our hymn singing can be vital and more meaningful even if you are running out of breath and you wish that darn organist would slow down — just a little. Cheer up! You may have to give up smoking to keep up, but soon you'll discover the true joy of singing musically and with understanding.

USING A HYMN AS AN ANTHEM

Take the hymn "Tell me the Old, Old Story" as an example. It could be sung in the following manner:

Verse 1:   Harmony

Verse 2:   Sopranos on words, everyone else humming until two lines before refrain, then all sing words in harmony.

Verse 3:   Unison first two lines, rest in harmony

Verse 4:   First two lines in harmony a capella with pause at end of each phrase ("Molto Freedom"). Organ joins in gradually, increasing in volume and speed. Rest SATB harmony, ritardando to end.

Another idea;

Verse 1:	Unison
Verse 2:	Harmony
Verse 3:	Ladies
Verse 4:	Harmony

or

Verse 1:	Harmony
Verse 2:	Unison with Faux Bourdon in organ
Verse 3:	Organ improvisation under choir in harmony
Verse 4:	Unison

APPENDIX A

Summary of the Qualifications
and Experience of (Your Name)

APPENDIX B

325 Main Street,
Winnipeg, Manitoba,
R3J 2X5
November 29, 19__ __

Mr. Smith,
Assiniboia United Church,
Assiniboia, Manitoba

Dear Sir,

I am replying to your advertisement of November 27 in the Winnipeg Free Press for the position of Director of Music at Assiniboia United Church. I enclose a summary of my qualifications and experience for your perusal.

    I have been Director of Music at Highlands United Church for the past three years and in that time I have organized a complete choral programme and was responsible for etc.

APPENDIX C

John George Smith
325 Main Street
Winnipeg, Manitoba
R3C 1A5
(203) 463-1986

Photo

31 years old
Born Winnipeg, Manitoba
Married to Mary Hammond
2 children.

APPENDIX D

CHRONOLOGY

1968 Assistant Conductor, Collegiate Singers, U of Manitoba
      (Conducted two concert performances)

1969 Organist and Choir Director, Grace United Church
      (Five choirs, instrumental programme, innovative services)

1970 Director of Music, Highlands United Church

APPENDIX E

Teaching Experience: 3 years Porter Elementary School, Grades 1-5

Administrative Responsibility: President, Student's Council

APPENDIX F

CONTRACT FOR CHURCH MUSICIANS

Date:

Effective on   ,and until the termination of this agreement

as hereinafter provided, (Name)   shall act as

(Title)   at (Church)

at a salary of $ per year, payable

This salary shall be reviewed annually at the time of the preparation of the church budget.

The above named person shall have the following duties and responsibilities:

1.   He shall provide organ music and direct the choir(s) at the services regularly scheduled
on   . He shall select appropriate organ and choral music for each
service.

2.   He shall provide organ and choral music for the following additional services during
the year:

3.   He shall have responsibility for the leadership of the following choirs:

4.   He shall rehearse once weekly (or as otherwise specified) with each of the choirs.
During the summer months the choir schedule shall be:

5.   He shall receive cooperation from the pastor and the music committee in the area of
general planning and leadership of the music program. He shall be directly responsible to:

APPENDIX F (cont'd.)

6.   He shall be responsible for the purchase of all necessary music and music supplies and the hiring of instrumental and vocal soloists. Expenditures in this area shall not exceed the amount provided in the church budget. The budget in the coming year for these expenses is $

7.   He shall be permitted to use the church facilities (organ, piano) for private teaching. Times of lessons and use of facilities must be scheduled in advance through the church office so as not to conflict with the church program needs. Students who use the church organ are expected to pay a fee to the church which shall be   per hour.

8.   His services shall be utilized at all weddings requiring organ music held within the church. The services of other organists may be used only with the permiss permission of the regular organist. In such cases the regular organist shall receive his normal wedding fee. For a short program of organ music preceding the wedding ceremony and performing at the wedding ceremony the fee shall be $. For attendance at the wedding rehearsal an additional fee shall be $. Additional remuneration shall be made for special music or if attendance at extra rehearsals is required.

9.   He shall provide music for funeral services held within the church if available at the time of the funeral. The fee for such a service shall be $

10.   He shall report to the appropriate committee the condition and needs for the maintenance of the church organ(s) and piano(s). The church shall provide money for the proper care of these instruments. Guest organists or recitalists shall not be permitted to use the church organ without prior approval of the regular organist.

11.   He shall be granted a vacation (with full salary) of   weeks annually. He shall assist the church in arranging for a substitute organist.

12.   He shall be eligible for   sick leave during the year. In such cases the church shall pay for the services of the substitute organist and/or director. Sick leave shall be taken only when his illness would prevent him from performing his regular duties. In case of extended illness the church should consider the granting of additional sick leave time.

13.   The church shall provide the following fringe benefits for the above named person and his family: Blue Cross/Blue Shield, Major Medical Insurance, Pension Plan, Life Insurance. These benefits shall take into account the person's needs and be commensurate with the benefits received by the other employees of the church.

14.   The church shall reimburse the above named person up to $ annually for expenses incurred by him in attending a church music conference, workshop or institute.

APPENDIX F (cont'd.)

15.   The above named person shall give notice of termination of his employment at least (90) days in advance of termination. The church should likewise give (90) days advance notice in the event they wish to terminate his employment.

Signature and Title of
Church Representative

Signature of Church Musician

APPENDIX G

HOURS SPENT TRAINING	5	5-10	10-15	15-20	20-25	25-30	35-40
Up to ten years General Musical Training (Private Lessons)	$1,000	$1,500	$2,000	$2,500	$3,200	$3,800	$5,000
Training as Above Plus Five Years Experience	1,500	2,500	3,500	4,500	5,500	7,000	8,000
Bachelor of Music	2,000	3,500	4,500	6,000	8,000	10,000	12,000
Master of Music	2,500	4,000	6,000	8,000	10,000	12,000	14,000

APPENDIX H

INFORMATION FORM

NAME:_____

ADDRESS: _____ AGE: _____

_____ PHONE: _____

OCCUPATION: _____

MUSICAL TRAINING: _____

_____

MUSICAL EXPERIENCE: _____

_____

APPENDIX I

PROPAGANDA CARD

WHAT KIND OF CHOIR MEMBER ARE YOU?

Tries to attend all rehearsals unless absolutely impossible.

Attends rehearsals unless something important comes up — like a TV program.

Phones conductor or attendance secretary if unable to attend.

Forgets about telling anyone about not going to rehearsal (They won't miss me anyway!).

Is seated, ready to sing, five minutes early.

Wanders in five minutes late and is noisy.

Has all necessary music and a pencil.

Jumps up to get music for every number, no pencil.

Asks to be excused from performance if unsure of music or too many rehearsals missed.

Expects to sing in the concert even though attendance has been poor and unsure of music.

Quiet and attentive.

Constantly talking.

Chews gum!

IT IS A SIMPLE MATTER OF GOOD MANNERS
AND CONSIDERATION FOR OTHERS.

APPENDIX J

ATTENDANCE RECORD

NOVEMBER DAY	2	9	16			
(Month) EVENT	R	R	C			
BROWN, Harry	✔	✔	✔			
SMITH, Mary	×	✔	✔			R = Rehearsal
						C = Concert

APPENDIX K

CHOIR POSTCARDS

REHEARSAL

WHEN? _____

WHERE? _____

REMINDER

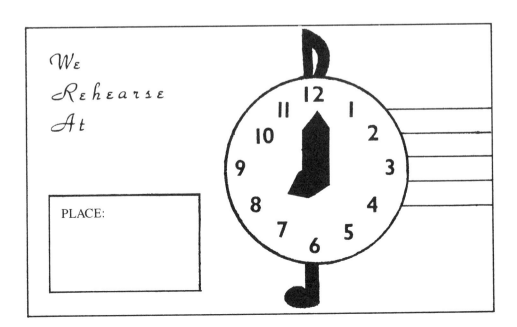

We Rehearse At

PLACE:

APPENDIX K (cont'd.)

APPENDIX K (cont'd.)

We missed you...

A CONCERT MEMO

DATE _____

TIME_____

PLACE _____

_____

APPENDIX L

FILE CARDS

Composer	Title
Resources	Language	Text
Publisher/No./Cost	Occasion
Period	Type of Piece
Timing	Difficulty	Ranges
Performance	Comments

Title	Composer/Editor
Resources	Language	Text
Publisher/No./Cost	Occasion
Period	Type of Piece
Timing	Difficulty	Ranges
Performance	Comments

APPENDIX M

PLANNING FOR THE YEAR

DATE		OCCASION	TITLE/COMPOSER	SOURCE
September	1	—	Prayer Of St. Richard Of Chichester — L.J. White	Oxford
	8	—	With A Voice Of Singing — Shaw	Boosey
	15	—	Print Thine Image — Johnson	Augsburg
	22	Family	Lord Of The Dance	Hymn Book
	29	—	David's Lamentation And Assurance — Billings	Schirmer
October	6	—	Joy Is Like The Rain — Winter	Vanguard
	13	Thanksgiving	Sing To The Lord Of Harvest — Willan	Concordia
	20	Communion	Sons Of God	Hymn Book
	27	Family	Worship The Lord In The Beauty Of Holiness	Hymn Book
November	3	All Saints	Sine Nomine — Vaughan Williams	Oxford
	10	Remembrance	Let Us Now Praise Famous Men — Vaughan Williams	Hymn Book
	17	—	Ride The Chariot — Smith	Kjos
	24	—	Guest Soloist	
December	1	Advent	Gloria — Dufay	Marks
	8	Family	Every Star Shall Sing A Carol	Hymn Book
	15	Advent	Lullay My Liking — Holst	Schirmer
	22	Advent	What Is This Lovely Fragrance? — Willan	Thompson
	25	Christmas	Christmas Day — Holst	Oxford
	29	—	In The Bleak Midwinter	Hymn Book
January	5	—	Christ Whose Glory Fills The Skies — Willan	Concordia
	12	—	Morning Has Broken — Stevens	Pop Song
	19	Family	Old Hundredth — Vaughan Williams	Oxford
	26	—	In The Garden (Duet)	Gospel Song
February	2	—	Non Nobis Domine — Byrd	Round
	9	Communion	Come Holy Ghost	Hymn Book
	16	—	Tune Thy Music To Thy Heart — Rowley	Schirmer
	23	—	Spirit Of God (Morecambe)	Hymnary
March	2	—	Zaccheus — Winter	Vanguard
	9	—	Guest Soloist	

APPENDIX M (cont'd.)

DATE		OCCASION	TITLE/COMPOSER	SOURCE
March	16	Communion	Let Us Break Bread	Hymn Book
	23	Palm Sunday	Rejoice In The Lord Always — Purcell (Instrumentalists)	Oxford
	28	Good Friday	When Jesus Wept — Billings	Round
	30	Easter	Hallelujah, Amen — Handel	Schirmer
April	6	—	Hymn To The Unknown God — Holst	Oxford
	13	Family	Sing We Of The Modern City	Hymn Book
	20	—	Gloria In Excelsis — Mozart	Harris
	27	—	Guest Soloist	
May	4	—	Here Is Thy Footstool — Creston	Schirmer
	11	—	Dear Lord And Father — Parry	Oxford
	18	Communion	God Reveals His Presence	Hymn Book
	25	—	They'll Know We Are Christians By Our Love	Hymns For Now
June	1	—	Ave Verum — Mozart	Harris
	8	—	Fight The Good Fight — Rhodes	Oxford
	15	—	We Praise Thee, O God — Willan	Concordia
	22	—	How Firm A Foundation	Hymn Book
	29	—	Lead Me, Lord — Wesley	Schirmer
July August			Guest Soloists	

APPENDIX N
SAMPLE PROGRAMME

St. Stephen's-on-the-Hill
United Church

IT'S A

GRAND NIGHT

for

SINGING!

Friday, May 1st, 1970

APPENDIX N (cont'd.)

O CANADA arr. Godfrey Ridout
Junior Choir:

Lord of the Dance arr. Sydney Carter
It's a Long Road to Freedom Medical Mission Sisters
Happiness (from "You're a Good Man, Charlie Brown") Gesner
DO RE MI (from "The Sound of Music") Rodgers and Hammerstein
      *DO a deer, a female deer
       RE a drop of Golden sun
       MI a name I call myself
       FA a long, long way to run
       SO a needle pulling thread
       LA a note to follow SO
       TI a drink with jam and bread
       That will bring us back to DO

Miss Isabel Rodriguez:

The More I See You Harry Warren
A Time for Us (from "Romeo and Juliet") Nino Rota
Sweet Caroline Neil Diamond
The Look of Love Bacharach
Traces Buie/Cobb/Gordy

Senior Choir

Gloria Patri Palestrina
He, Watching Over Israel Mendelssohn
Bless the Lord, O My Soul Ippolitof-Ivanov
Battle Hymn of the Republic arr. Steffe
      *Glory! Glory! Hallelujah!
       Glory! Glory! Hallelujah!
       Glory! Glory! Hallelujah!
       His Truth is marching on!

INTERMISSION

*Audience is invited to join in the singing

APPENDIX N (cont'd.)

Four times Six plus One

I Believe	Drake
59th Street Bridge Song (Feelin' Groovy)	Paul Simon
Good Morning Starshine (from "Hair")	Galt MacDermot

Even Stephens

All Through the Night	Welsh Traditional
Let There be Peace on Earth	Miller & Jackson
Turn Around, Look at Me	Jerry Capehart
Teddy Bears' Picnic	John Bratton
(Starring Bill & Mac, Staged by Howard Sweezie)	

Senior Choir

Come to Me, Bend to Me (from "Brigadoon")	Lerner and Loewe
Younger than Springtime (from "South Pacific")	Rodgers and Hammerstein
It's a Grand Night for Singing (from "State Fair")	Rodgers and Hammerstein

    *It's a grand night for singing! The moon is flying high
    And somewhere a bird who is bound he'll be heard
    Is throwing his heart at the sky.
    It's a grand night for singing! The stars are bright above,
    The earth is aglow and to add to the show,
    I think I am falling in love.
    Falling, falling in love.**

Maybe it's more than the moon, Maybe it's more than the birds
Maybe it's more than the sight of the night in a light too lovely for words.
Maybe it's more than the earth, shiny in silvery blue,
Maybe the reason I'm feeling this way has something to do with you!

Repeat from * to **

Refreshments will be served in the Common Room.

APPENDIX N (cont'd.)

MUSIC DIRECTOR: Wayne Gilpin, Mus. Bac.

Junior Choir:	CGIT:	Senior Choir:
L. BENNETT	D. DERSCH	SHIRLEY NOLTIE
M. REID	P. BEGLEY	Mary Wood
Bruce	E. BALDWIN	Grace Stoll
Doug	E. CHESSMAN	Barb Woodburn
Brant	Nancy B.	Isobel Greenfield
Scott	Nancy C.	Airlie Suutari
David	Kathy N.	Claire Macdonald
Nancy	Kelly N.	Laurie Bennett
Susan B.	Cathy I.	Jane Brown
Kathy	Carol D.	Karen Heikkila
Jennifer	Carolyn M.	Marj McNaughton
Sylvia	Joanne U.	Barbara Johnston
Lynn	Mary W.	Ted Dersch
Kirsti	Holly P.	Roger Bolt
Wendy	Mary Ellen S.	Mac Norris
Christy	Sherry S.	John Porteous
Susan F.	Debbie F.	Bill McNaughton
Cindy	Jill N.	
	Kim P.	**Men's Group**
THANKS TO	Debbie P.	BILL McNAUGHTON
EVERYONE WHO	Bev E.	Howard Angus
HELPED MAKE	Janet C.	Mac Norris
IT A "GRAND	Susan C.	Howard Sweezie
NIGHT FOR	Susy T.	Ted Dersch
SINGING"	Leslie C.	Ron Gauley
	Cathy A.	John Bower
	Arlene P.	Jack Chessman
	Rosemary M.	Roger Bolt
	Janet M.	John Porteous
		Dave Burstow

48

APPENDIX O

SAMPLE TIMETABLE

	SUNDAY	MONDAY	TUESDAY	WEDNESDAY	THURSDAY	FRIDAY	SATURDAY
9	Men's Group						Private Teaching
10	Pre-Service Rehearsal		Study, Preparation, Practicing				
11	Sunday Service						
12	Lunch						
1-2	High School Choir						Weddings
3							
4-6		Private Teaching	Primary Choir	Private Teaching	Private Teaching		
7-9	Private Teaching (Theory)		Private Teaching	Ladies Group	Junior Choir Senior Choir (8-10)		